Commemorating 100 Years of

St. Nicholas Church

A History . . .

ISBN: 978-1-990265-04-4

The Congregation of St. Nicholas Russo-Greek Orthodox Church

First Edition: November 2000
Second Edition: May 2021

Additional Copies may be purchased from:
W.C.H.F.
#374-9768-170 Street
Edmonton, Alberta
CANADA,   T5T 5L4

Price: $15.95

Typeset and Printed by
Heritage Books – Canada
#374, 9768-170 Street
Edmonton, Alberta
Canada, T5T 5L4

Credits:

Photography

- Special Event- 100th Anniversary Celebration Day
    Reuben A. Bauer - *Photos by Rubens'* Photo Studio
    Edmonton, Alberta

- Special Photo Submissions
    Gladys Gammon, Eugene Topolnisky, Bill Topolnitsky,
    Alexander Plesko

- Historic Photos
    Alexander Plesko, Bill Topolnitsky, Eugene Topolnisky

Historical Research

- Alexander Plesko - *Prologue*

- Eugene Topolnisky - *The Two Queens*

- Alexander Plesko - Section I - Captions to historical photos

- Father Evan Lowig - Section II - Captions to the Special
    100th Anniversary Day Event

Printing, Publishing, Design

- Marcon Consulting - Publishing, Edmonton, Alberta

- Reuben A. Bauer - Designing

Her Majesty Queen Victoria

In this publication. the Ukrainian people of the Wostok-Bukowina Church and community are reminded of the historical role and significance of Queen Victoria in their lives. By the benevolent act of the great Queen, the Ukrainian immigrants that migrated to the north-eastern part of Alberta, Canada, then as now, hold Her Majesty in very high regard and respect for the invaluable assistance that she personally provided in the process of opening up the negotiation with the Austrian Empire by releasing these immigrants to come to Canada and build a new life.

Reverence and deep affection for the Monarchy is maintained in the present Ukrainian-Canadian cultural heritage for this most generous act. "Since our present ruler, Queen Elizabeth II, is both descended from that great monarch and as well our current sovereign, the Ukrainian people wish to identify themselves with this historic link. It is with humble gratitude and thanksgiving that we graciously wish to acknowledge Her Majesty Queen Elizabeth II in this very special way. " - *Eugene Topolnisky*

Her Majesty Queen Elizabeth II

Prologue

One Hundred Years ...
A History of St. Nicholas
Russo-Greek Orthodox Church

by Alexander Plesko

In the latter part of the eighteenth century, there was an extensive migration of various groups of people from central Europe to the prairie flatlands of western Canada. Whatever district these groups settled in, they fulfilled a great desire, that of having churches of their particular faith built near them.

One such group that located itself out west near Wostok, Alberta built a church in 1900 naming it Bukowina St. Nicholas Church of Russo-Greek Orthodox extraction. The members of the original committee were: Mr. Ballan, Hnat Babich, Gregory Wasylynchuk, George Klapatiuk, Wasyl Topolnisky, Tom Tkachuk, Dmetro Melenka, Nykolai Topolnitsky and John Scraba.

Our church has its early beginnings in the late 1890's with the site chosen beside the South Fork Victoria Trail.

The church is a one-storey, log, shingle-roofed building and is 28 feet wide and 45 feet long. Local material was used in the construction. Huge logs, all cut and hewn by hand were hauled in from local forests and set on a foundation of rocks and stones from the local fields. It took three years of hard labour and determination to complete it.

In the summer of 1900 the church was blessed and the first service held. The name St. Nicholas was chosen for the Saint who was famous for great deeds in helping the needy. Services in the early years of our church were sporadic and conducted by missionaries from the Russo Greek Orthodox Church.

There is nothing in the records to show whether the land where the church was built was donated, but in 1903 the first payment was made to the C.P.R. for forty-seven acres including the land where the church stands at the present time. Last payment on this land was made in June of 1909.

The trustees at that time were Ivan T. Tkachuk, Elias Soloniuk and Gregory Wasylynchuk. Other known members of the church were George Klapatiuk, Theodore Kushneriuk, Evan Kozakewich, Gawrelo Andriats. Evan Ballan, Wasyl Tyminski, Evan Maga, Wasyl Topolnisky, Hnat Babich and Dmytri Melenka.

Shortly after the construction of the church was completed, a sixteen foot by eighteen foot Belfry was built of logs. The Belfry was renovated in 1922 to house the new bell which was purchased from the Meneely Bell Co. of Troy, New York for the sum of $422.00. The bell is made of the finest brands of new Lake Superior copper and new imported tin and guaranteed against fracture of tone for 15 years. There was no duty, at that time, on bells entering Canada (for church purposes) from the United States, so the bell was delivered prepaid to Lamont.

In the summer of 1939, the members decided to update the church. They hired Anton Punka to enlarge the vestibule. tear the siding off the walls and put two ply paper on them, fix the windows, put in doors and build stairs. They excavated under the church and laid a concrete foundation and made a basement.

Another man, Nick Nickifore, was hired to put stucco on the church and vestibule and he quoted his price at 35 cents a square yard, so for 295 yards he was paid $103.25. (Consider what the price would be now). In the 1940's, Adam Hurda put in a new hardwood floor in the church.

In 1954 the church was painted, the ceiling blue with white stars, the walls and windows white with blue casings and the altar doors in gold. The floor was sanded and varnished. Peter Wasylynchuk, Mike Kushneriuk and Harry Shopik were the painting committee.

Electric Power was brought into the church in late 1967. Nychka Electric from Lamont did the wiring.

The committee of the year 1975 consisted of Peter Wasylynchuk, President, Metro Hackman, Secretary, and John Kozakewich, Treasurer. Mr. Peter Wasylynchuk who is a third generation pillar in this church, had served as chairman of the church board for twenty-five years. His grandfather, Gregory, was one of the original founders; his father Nicholas was also a constant throughout the years as are Peter's son and daughter who are fourth generation adherents.

The first priest to serve in our church was Rev. Alexandr Antoniev. The priest who served us most recently was Rev. Evan Lowig.

The current board for the year 2000 consists of Bill Kozak.ewich as chairman, Sylvia Halicki, Secretary Treasurer, and Alexander Plesko, as Vice Chairman. Directors are Donald Topolnisky, Jim Gammon, Elias Kozakewich and Bill Topolnitsky.

Contents

Section I

Section II

Founding Members of Bukowina Church
(Back Row L-R) Sam and Nykolai; (Front Row L-R) Hrehorey and Wasyl sons of Ivan and Aksenia Topolnitsky.

Maria and Wasyl Topolnisky

George Krawchuk, (original members of Bukowina Church) with
Mr. & Mrs. Zachowsky.

Eli and Helen Tanasiuk, Mary, Doris and Lil.   Original Members of
Bukowina Church.

Father Alexander Kamenov with early parishioners.

Wasyl and Katerina (Babich) Marian. (Original Members of
Bukowina Church.

Dmytri Hackman
He is the father of Nickolai Hackman.

Bukowina Church Elders at the 90th Anniversary, July 15th, 1990.
Eli Klompas, Paul Kubersky and John Hancheruk.

One of the original members Martha Dudar and her daughter on the right side.

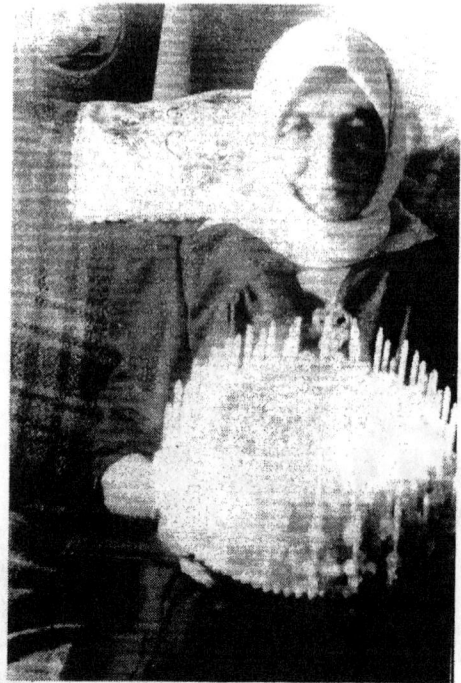

Annie (Rochmistruk) Topolnitsky wife of Nykolai Topolnitsky. Here she is celebrating her birthday of nearly a century. She was one of the earliest of the pioneering people in the area of Wostok.

Wasyl and Maria Topolnisky and their daughters.
(L-R) Eva Hunter, Wasyl, Maria, Annie Drabiuk, Katie Shopik,
Elsie Wasylynchuk, Sophie Frunchak, Eugenia Plesko, Pearl Bouyea,
Lena Albiston, Mary Stewart and Dorothy Tanasiuk at Bukowina
Church n 1951.

Another pioneering family of the Wostok community.

More early pioneers of the area.

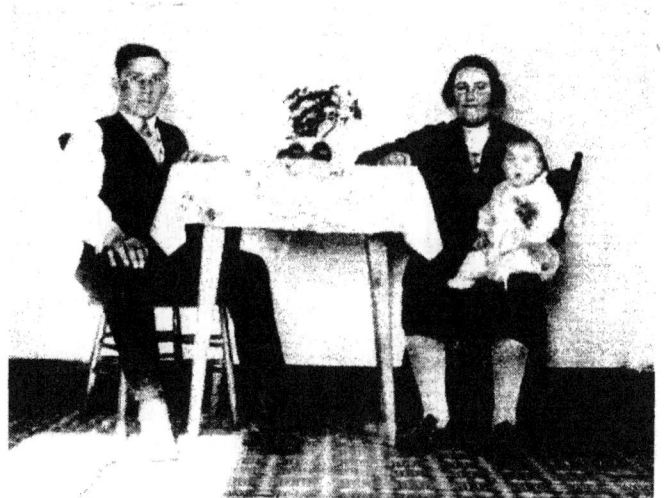

Nickolai Hackman and wife Rose with their daughter Eva. Nicholai
was the former Secretary of St. Nicholas Church in the 1930's.

Form 502-92

PROVINCE OF ALBERTA 966

CANADA

Certificate of Incorporation

I Hereby Certify that

The ....

is this day incorporated under "The Religious Societies' Lands Act" of the Province of Alberta.

Given under my hand and seal of office at Edmonton, Alberta, this ..... 19 ..... day of ..... AUGUST ..... A.D. 19 60.

(SEAL, &c.)
Registrar of Joint Stock Companies

Certificate of Incorporation

БЛАГОСЛОВЕННАЯ Грамота

Американской и Банадской Спархіи

Церковному Старостѣ Св. Николаевской церкви въ н. Востокѣ /Альберта, Канада/

Василію ТОПОЛЬНИЦКОМУ

Преподается Божіе благословеніе по случаю 50-лѣтія со дня основанія Св. Николаевской церкви въ н. Востокѣ. Да вознаградитъ Господь вѣрнаго церковнаго труженика и да даруетъ ему и его семьѣ благосостояніе въ сей жизни и вѣчное спасеніе въ жизни будущей.

+ Архіепископъ Виталій.-

9/22 сентября 1951 года

Викарній Епископъ

Ewan Hancheruk and Wasyl Topolnisky were recognized for their 50 years of Altar Service at St. Nicholas Church. Wasyl received this certificate on Sept. 22, 1951.

Duplicate Certificate of Title.

Refer Cert. No. 196 C.I.R.

Last Value $500

North Alberta Land Registration District.

This is to Certify that the Board of Trustees for the Congregation of the Orthodox Russo-Greek Catholic Church at Wostok, in the Province of Alberta, in the Dominion of Canada

is now the owner of an estate in fee simple

of and in all that portion of the North West quarter of section Sixteen (15) of Township Fifty-six (56) Range Seventeen (17) West of the Fourth Meridian, in the said Province, lying North of a roadway One Chain in width in the said North West quarter section Sixteen (15) the Southerly and Easterly limits of which are described as follows: commencing at a point in the West boundary of the said quarter section being the intersection ...

THE TITLES ACT, Sec. 42. — The land mentioned in any certificate of title granted under this Act shall be subject by implication without any special mention therein, unless the contrary is expressly declared, to certain exceptions ... [small print margin text]

Here is the duplicate Certificate of Title issued by the Land Registration District of Alberta to the Congregation of Russo-Greek Orthodox Church at Wostok.

As the pioneering farmers were breaking the land, they needed first to clear off the logs. These logs were brought to a saw-mill to be cut and trimmed into lumber for the construction of homes, farm buildings and this case the church. Here the men of the congregation are busily engaged in cutting logs as they prepare to build the church.

Trimming the logs to make boards. (L-R) Bill N. Topolnitsky, Anne Topolnitsky, Harry Topolnitsky, unknown lady and John Topolnitsky.

The trim that comes off the logs is called, "slabs". These slabs were then cut into firewood.

A close-up view of farmers using a "planer", an instrument used to cut the bark off of trees and make straight boards for building.

After the church was built, it was consecrated. The Bishop and Priest along with the congregation walked around the building blessing the new structure.

----->>

The Wostok Orthodox Church was ready for occupancy in 1900. This was Bukowina Church, circa early 1940's.

<<-----------

This is Bukowina-Wostok St. Nicholas Church today.

<<------------

50th Anniversary at Wostok Church
Ewan Hancheruk, Rev. Seraphim and Rev. Varchol.

Priest Wasyl Boyko with Catechism Class.

50th Anniversary of Wostok Church
(L-R) Maria Topolnisky, Marena Kozakewich, Nicholai
Kozakewich, Rev. T. Varchol, Matushka Varchol, Rev. Seraphim
of St. Vladimir's Cathedral , Ewan Hancheruk, Wasyl Topolnisky
and Iwan Marian.

Priest Wasyl Boyko with the Ladies of the Bukowina Church.

Priest Wasyl Boyko with the men
of Bukowina Church.
<<---------

The Diamond Jubilee of Bukowina Church
Elias Kozakewich, Fr. Arch Deacon Andrew,
His Grace Bishop Joasaph, Parish Priest Wasyl
Ostashek, Matushka Ostashek, Michael, Ralph and
Jimmy Kozakewich, John Tkachuk and Bill
Kozakewich, November 2nd, 1975. ------->>

80th Anniversary - August 24th 1980
(Bottom Row L-R) Katie Wasylynchuk,
Eugenia   Plesko, Jenny Wasylynchuk, Ann
Klapatiuk, Matushka Ostashek, Florence
Kozakewich, Cassie Kozakewich, (Second
Row L-R) Nancy Tanasichuk, Mary Olinek,
Peter Wasylynchuk, Emma Kubersky, Rose
Yakoweshen, John Kozakewich. (Third
Row: L-R) Alexander Plesko, Steve Olinek,
Rev. Ostashek, Steve Klaptiuk, Paul
Kubersky, Nick Yakoweshen, Pat Gubersky.
<<---------

90th Anniversary Dinner At Wostok Hall
Sub Deacons John Woodrofe, John Panasiuk, John
Scratch, Priest Larry Reinheimer, His Grace Bishop
Seraphim, Priest Orest Oleksky, President Fred
Wasylynchuk and Secretary Bill Kozakewich.
<<-------------

90th Anniversary July 15th 1990
(Bottom Row L-R) Mary Andruchow, Eli
Klompas, Ann Kapatuik, John Hancheruk,
Cassie Kozakewich, (Second Row L-R) Fred
Wasylynchuk, Eugenia Plesko, Katie
Klompas, Mary Bodnarek, Jenny Wasylynchuk,
Nancy Andreas, Nancy Topolnisky. (Third Row L-R)
Nick Bodnarek, Paul Kubersky, Katie
Wasylynchuk, Emma Kubersky. ----------------->>

The 100th Anniversary celebrations and
members of the congregation of St. Nicholas.

<<----------

Blessing graves "Provode" 1961
Archpriest Andrew Kokolsky and Peter Wasylynchuk

Provode Service - 1982
Rev. Ostashek, Alexander Plesko and Michael Kozakewich.

Priest Andrew Morbey, Matushka Alexandra and Patrick Stewart
(As St. Nicholas) giving gifts to the children. Dec. 19, 1989.

Good Friday -1998
Fred Wasylynchuk with the wooden mallets. The wooden mallets
were used instead of the bells which are silenced on Good Friday.

16

Good Friday Service - 1998
The carrying of the Shroud around the church.

Purchase Agreement between St. Nicholas Church and Meneely Bell Co. of the new church bell.

The new bell was purchased in 1922

17

Priest Larry Reinheimer blessing Gospel and Apostal Books,
donated by Mrs. Eugenia Plesko.

Blessing Paska at St. Nicholas Church (Bukowina) in the early
1900's.

Pictured here are Bishop Seraphim and Rev. Evan Lowig.

Priest Rev. Michael Andruchow

Rev. Fr. Alexander Kamenov

One of the early priests to serve St. Nicholas Church
was Rev. Fr. Anton Zeminoff.

Priest Nickolas Germogen serving a "Panachyda" (the memorial Service for the deceased).

Bishop Nikon's Visit - 1953
(L-R) Ewan Hancheruk, Bishop Nikon and Harry Halkow.

Rev. Andrew Morbey, June 10, 1990 who served at Wostok Church. This picture was taken at Desjarlais Church.

(Front Row L-R) .... Bishop Seraphim and Fr. Larry Reinheimer.

Weddings, Baptisms and Anniversaries

John and Mary (Shopik) Moisey married Feb. 6, 1942. Priest Theodore Varchol officated.

Tom and Marie (Kozakewich) Salahub married Feb. 20, 1960. Priest Fr. Wasyl Boyko officiated.

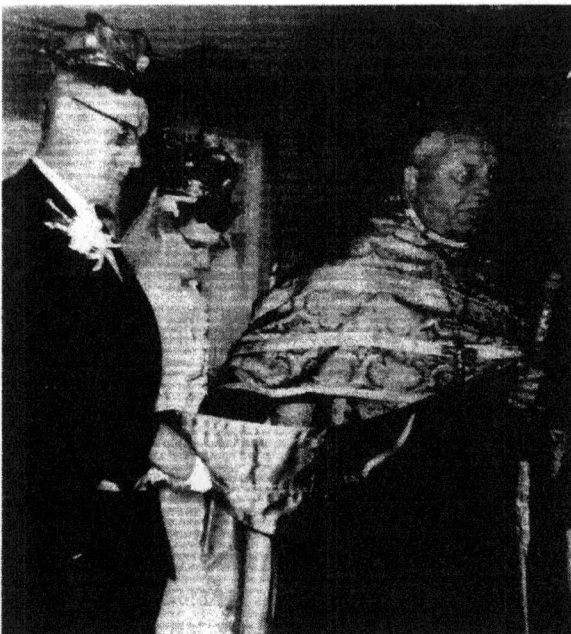

Bill and Kay (Baidak) Topolnitsky married June 17, 1960. Priest John Kowalchuk officiated.

(L-R) Alex Cholak, Kay and Bill Topolnitsky and Katie Sikora.

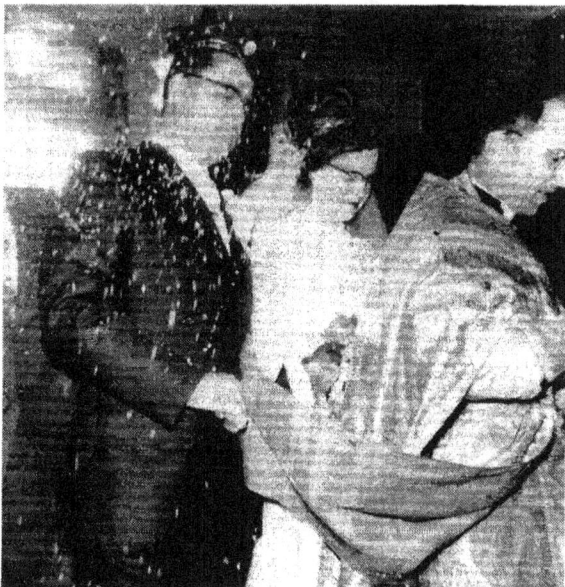

Ted and Nancy (Huley) Topolnistsky married July 26, 1956. Priest Vasily Hochachka officiated.

Nick and Elizabeth Topolnitsky Wedding Party at Wostok Church.

John and Lena (Philipchuk) Topolnitsky on their 50th Wedding Anniversary.

Nick and Elizabeth (Debrinsky) Topolnitsky.

Nick and Elizabeth (Debrinsky) Topolnitsky. Married June 29th 1957. Priest John Kowalchuk officiated.

Bill and Sylvia (Wasylynchuk) Farrus. Married on May 30th 1958. Priest Rev. John Kowalchuk officiated.

Peter and Katie Wasylynchuk 50th Anniversary - 1983.

Paul and Emma (Matenchuk) Kubersky. Married February 9th 1939. Priest Theodore S. Varkhol Officiated. Instead of confetti, streamers and rice were thrown at the Bride and Groom.

Marriage of Irene (Kozakewich) and Bill Zucht. Their wedding date was February 1969.
<<----------

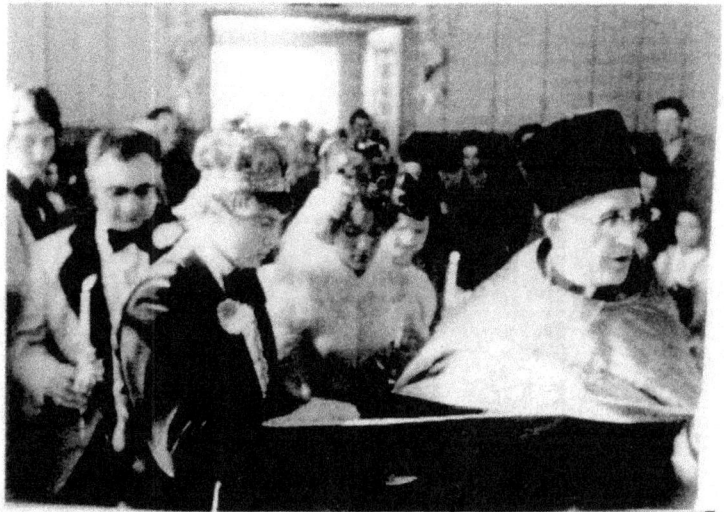

Marriage of Elias and Tammy (Petras) Kozakewich. Priest Wasyl Osteshek officiated.   ----------->>

(L-R) William and Cassie Kozakewich, Irene (Kozakewich) and Bill Zucht and Dorothy and Walter Zucht.
<<----------

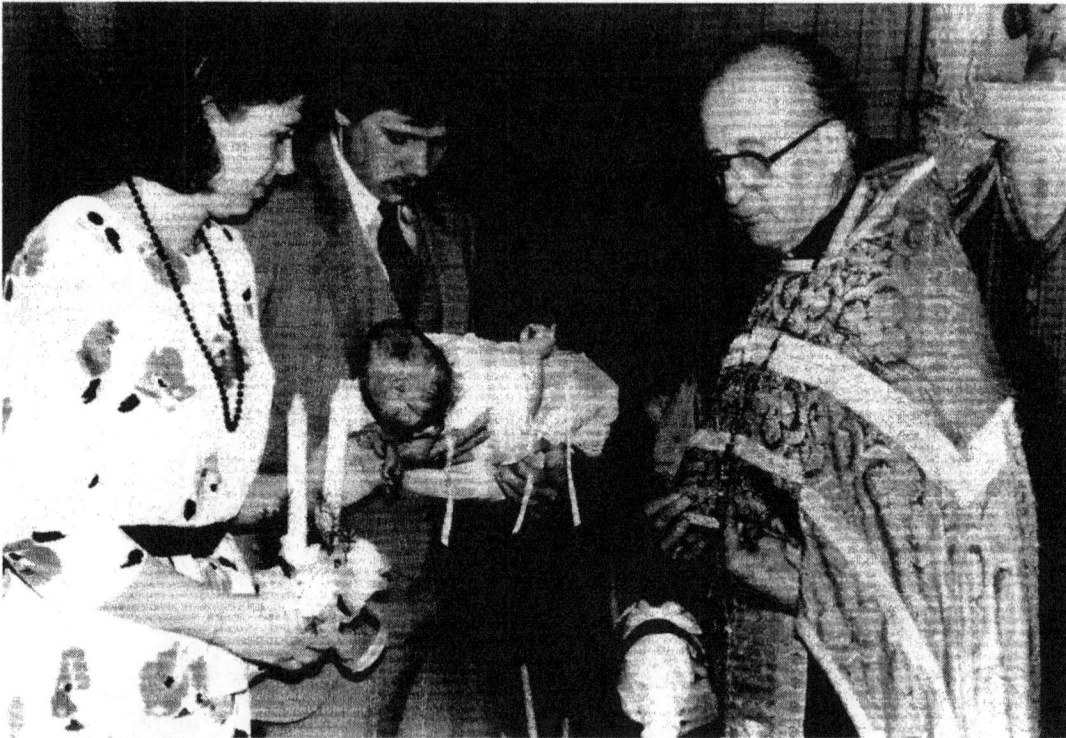

Rev. William Ostashek baptizing Lacey Kozakewich. God parents
were Colleen Petras and Michael Kozakewich.

The 80th Wostok Church Anniversary - August 24, 1980
Seated at head table (L-R) George and Verna Topolnisky. Priest
Wasyl Ostashek and Matushka Lena.

A Funeral Hearse
This was the funeral of Mrs. Maria
Gubersky who passed away on Feb.
12, 1941 at the age of 73 years.

<<------

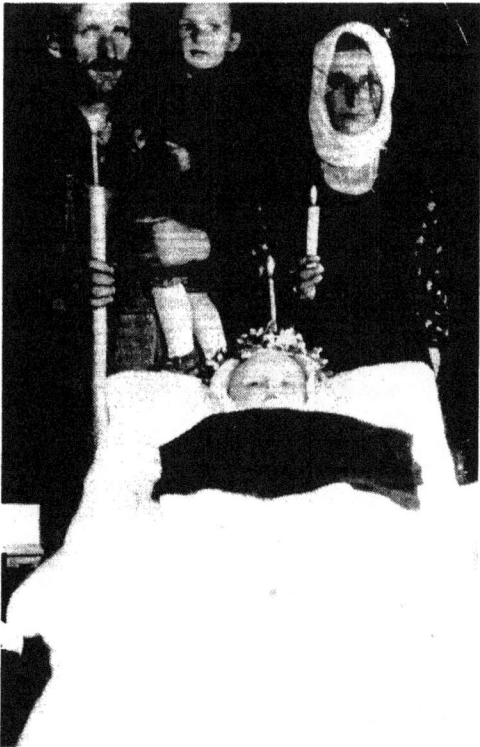

Nick and Helen (Topolnitsky) Kyca at the funeral of one of their
children.

One of the funerals where two children in one family passed away.
The mortality rate for young children in the early days was very
high. Many children died at an early age because of diptheria,
small-pox, while others were over-come by the "Spanish Influenza"
of 1918-1919 period.

26

Rev. Varchol officiating at the funeral of Paul Gubersky who passed away on Oct. 13, 1941 at the age of 83 years.

The home of Sam Topolnicky who raised a variety of pigeons. He also raised the now extinct "Carrier Pigeons" which he used to send messenges to let family members know when he was going to be arriving home by train.

The funeral of Egnat Plesko, June 1944.

A small farm home with a typcial "lean-to". The lean-to was like an after thought addition to the main part of the house, due to the increased need for space because of an increase in the family or a sign of financial betterment.

A partly finished 2-storey home in the area of Wostok. It was plastered with mud and straw mixed by hand and applied by hand. This mud plastering process was done to keep the building warm in winter and cool in summer.

<<------

As the pioneers improved their homesteads so did came the improvement of homes and living quarters. This illustration serves as another example of a fine home built by Ukrainian settlers in the early days.

------------->>

As their financial status improved, so did their homes. This was another very fine home. A very stylish modern home using "siding", (smooth home-cut boards) to cover the walls of the house. Usually these siding were painted to protect against weathering.

<<-----------------

Plowing the fields with steel-wheel tractors which had "lugs" on them provided the necessary traction in doing the field work. Here we see two local farmers doing their "field work", in this case plowing with two Case tractors.

<<------------

Horse power in the days before tractors were used was a common site.

-------------------->>

Horses used in grading the roads. This was usually done after some heavy rains and there were a lot of ruts. The road grader filled in the ruts and smoothed the dirt and/or gravel roads to make driving more comfortable.
<<---------------

Mixed farming was very common practice
in the early days. The early pioneers
needed a little bit of everything in order to
feed themselves for survival. So it was
necessary to raise all the farm animals.

<<-------------

A grain-grinder used by John Topolnitsky who did
custom work in the neighborhood. They would grind
up the grain for "chop" (a kind of mash) to field the
farm animals. This chop was more easily digestible
for animals and a real treat for them.

---------------------->>

Here are a group of men engaged in a
"farming bee", that is they are helping out
someone possibly in the threshing time. Usally
the farmer's wife prepared a noon-day lunch
which was taken out the fields for the
workmen.

<<----------------------

Before the days of the combine, threshing was done with a threshing machine otherwise known as a separator. The threshing machine was powered by a steam engine.

Early Transportation

To carry farm products to market a horse and buggy or also a "democrat" was used.

Crossing the North Saskatchewan River was no easy task. The early pioneers developed a "ferry boat" which was guided across the river by a heavy cable as the swift flowing water moved the ferry and all its cargo across the water. This was the Pakan Ferry.

Bill Topolnitsky seated at the rear of his first car, a Model "T"
Ford. He is taking his friends and neigbhors out for a ride. (L-R) Bill
Topolnitsky (on rear fender), Eli Hunchuk, unknown, John Hunchuk
(standing in the vehicle).

Other vehicles soon became popular. Here is a Model "A" Ford car
used for transportation of local families to go to church, visits, and
of course to the "big city" for that once year big shopping trip.

Section II
100 Year Celebration
1900 - 2000

Part of the Wostok Congregation awaits the arrival of the Bishop prior to the celebration of the Divine Liturgy on the centenary Feast Day.

Upon arrival at the church gate, Bishop Seraphim exchanges the kiss of peace with one of the altar servers.

Arrival of some of the celebrating clergy. Fr. Dennis Pihach, Rector of St. Herman's Orthodox Church in Edmonton and Chancellor of the Archdiocese of Canada (Orthodox Church in America), together with Deacon Andrew Piasta..

Bishop Seraphim puts on his mantle or Mantiya on his way to the temple. The Mantiya is a sign of monasticism, while the decorations are emblems of the episcopal office.

Greeted by the laity of St. Nicholas Church, Bishop Seraphim venerates the icon of St. Nicholas, Archbishop of Myra in Lycia (280-342), the patron of the temple and protector of the Western Ukrainian people including the Bukowinians.

Bishop Seraphim, accompanied by altar servers, is about to enter the St. Nicholas Russo-Greek Orthodox Church at Wostok as its Father in Christ.

The processional of lay people, altar servers and Bishop Seraphim makes its way from the churchyard gate to the doors of the temp where the Pontifical Divine Liturgy for the 100th Anniversary is about to be celebrated.

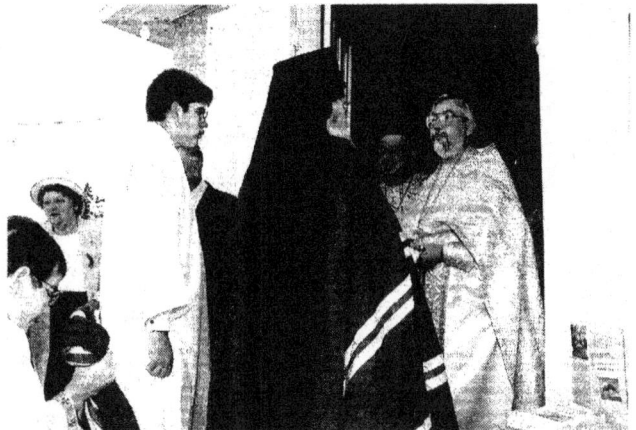

Fr. Evan Lowig, the rector of the St. Nicholas Russo-Greek Orthodox Church of Wostok-Bukowina greets Bishop Seraphim and asks for his prayers on behalf of the parish community at the doors of the temple.

Flanked by Deacon Andrew Piasta, Bishop Seraphim makes his entrance prayers before the Royal Doors of the inconostas (Icon screen) which separates the altar or sanctuary from the nave. In the foreground we see the concelebrating priests: Frs. Dennis Pihach, Vasyl Kolega and Evan Lowig.

After being fully vested, Bishop Seraphim blesses the congregation with special candlesticks known as the "Trikiri" and the "Dikiri". The Trikiri symbolizes the 3 persons of the one Godhead, Father, Son and Holy Spirit; while the Dikiri represents the 2 natures of Jesus Christ, human and divine.

Altar servers blessed to act as sub-deacons for the occasion of vesting Bishop Seraphim before the Liturgy begins.

Bishop Seraphim prays for the descent of the Holy spirit just prior to the Liturgy.

Bishop Seraphim blessing the processional banners which were made by Matushka (Priest's wife) Wasylyna (Lena) Ostashek for the Wostok-Bukowina Centennial. Her husband and Fr. Wasyl (Bill) Ostashek served the St. Nicholas Church from 1969 to 1987. He died in 1998 at age 85.

Entrance with the Gospel during the Divine Liturgy.

Bishop Seraphim standing in the center of the church during the Divine Liturgy prior the entrance with the Gospel.

Holding the Trikiri and Dikiri, Bishop Seraphim makes a reverential bow during the singing of the entrance hymn "Come, let us worship and fall down before Christ".

His Grace, the Right Reverend Seraphim, Bishop of Ottawa and the Archdiocese of Canada (Orthodox Church in America) was born in Edmonton, Alberta on January 25, 1946. He studied at the University of Alberta, Vancouver School of Theology and St. Vladimir's Seminary (New York). He was consecrated as auxiliary Bishop, June 13, 1987 and enthroned as ruling Bishop October 28, 1990.

Bishop Seraphim censing the congregation as the entrance hymn is completed with the verse, "Save us, Son of God, who rose from the dead. Save us we sing to you: Alleluia."

Holding the dikirion and the cross, Bishop Seraphim blesses the congregation with the words "Look down from heaven, O Lord and see, and visit this vineyard which has been planted by your right hand" accompanying the prayer, "Holy God, Holy Mighty, Holy Immortal have mercy on us."

Bishop Seraphim standing in front of the altar after the entrance with the Gospel has been completed.

Symbolizing the entrance into the heavenly sanctuary, Bishop Seraphim ascends to the high place behind the altar table.

Bishop Seraphim assisted at the High Place by Deacon Andrew Piasta and Reader Douglas Topolnitsky.

Bishop Seraphim in a reflective mood during his sermon.

Bishop Seraphim about to begin the sermon after the Gospel reading during the Pontifical Divine Liturgy on June 25th, 2000 at the Centennial celebration of the St. Nicholas Russo-Greek Orthodox Church of Wostok-Bukowina.

Bishop Seraphim in continuation of sermon as he delivers a challenging message to the congregation.

The congregation seated during Bishop Seraphim's sermon.

A close-up of Bishop Seraphim (born Kenneth Storheim) during the sermon at the Wostok 100th Anniversary Celebration.

Another perspective of the congregation and Bishop Seraphim's sermon.

Bishop Seraphim at the close of his sermon.

Bishop Seraphim praying just prior to the offertory procession with bread and wine that is known in the Byzantine Liturgy as the Great Entrance.

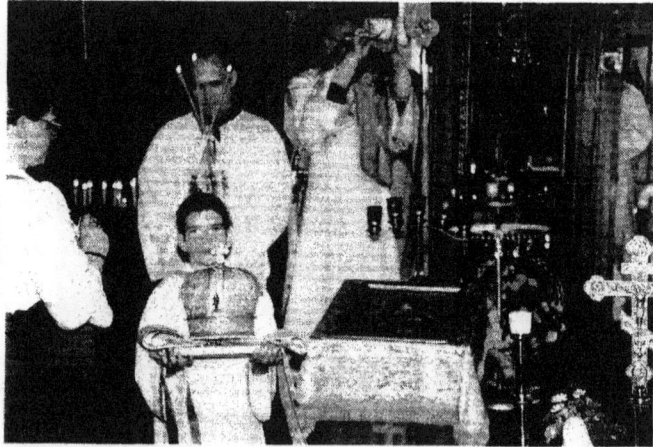

With discos or paten in hand, Bishop Seraphim commemorates the Primate of the Orthodox Church in America, His Beatitude, Metropolitan Theodosius.

The Great Entrance. Nicholas Topolnitsky holds the mitre on top of the Bishop's "omophor" (also known as the pallum, an ancient sign of episcopal authority) and service book. Serving as Sub-deacon, Reader David Lincoln carries the Trikiri. Deacon Andrew Piasta holds the discos or paten with the Eucharistic bread and commemorates followed by Bishop Seraphim.

Holding the chalice filled with wine (to which water has been added), Bishop Seraphim finishes commemorations at the Great Entrance.

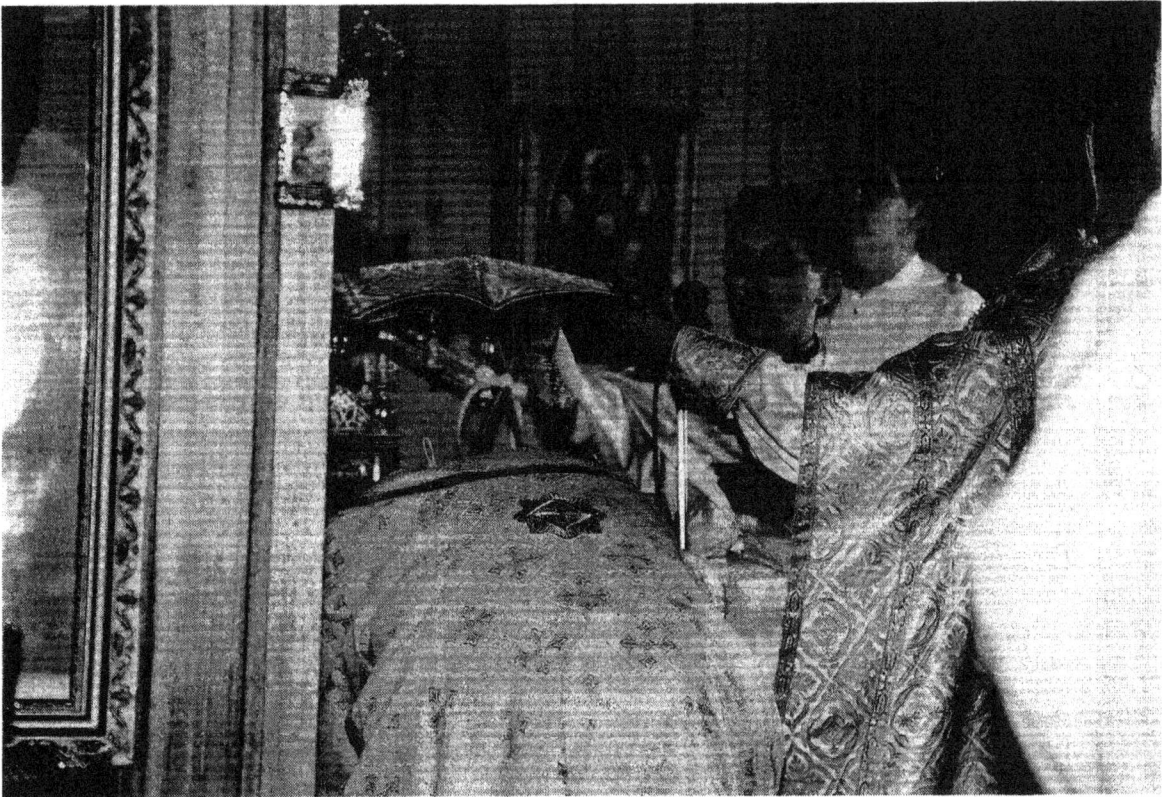

As the Nicaeo-Constantinopolitan Creed is sung, con-celebrating priests wave the air above the Bishop Seraphim. The air is a special cloth used to cover the Eucharistic gifts. The waving of the air was originally a practical gesture to which was given symbolic meaning, Le; the grace and operation of the Holy Spirit.

After the consecration of the Eucharistic gifts, Bishop Seraphim blesses the congregation with Trikiri and Dikiri. Orthodox Christians believe that the Holy Spirit transforms the Eucharistic gifts of Bread and Wine into the Body and Blood of Christ.

Bishop Seraphim facing the altar table shortly after the consecration of the Eucharistic gifts.

In many Orthodox churches during the communion of the clergy, the Royal Doors of the iconostas are closed and the curtain is drawn. Again this is something that originates in the practical need for peace and quiet but come to be connected with heightening the "Mysterium Fidei" - the Mystery of Faith.

Bishop Seraphim giving communion to Matushka Wasylyna Ostashek.

The communion of the laity is about to begin.

Bishop Seraphim giving communion to Evangeline Kosakewich who is the designated reader at the St. Nicholas Church of Wostok-Bukowina since 1997.

Bishop Seraphim administering communion to the younger generation of the parish.

Bishop Seraphim continuing in his distribution of Communion to the parishioners.

Bishop Seraphim giving communion to the older members of congregation. Receiving communion is Andrew Goroniuk who is the president of the Sunland Holy Trinity Orthodox Church (which is north and east of Andrew).

Bishop Seraphim giving communion to Alec (Oleksa) Shukalek who is the president of the St. Nicholas Greek Orthodox Church of Desjarlais (located north of Willingdon).

Bishop Seraphim distributing communion while those who have already received are about to take a sip of water as a post-communion absolution.

To accommodate the large numbers of people on the June 25th anniversary day, there were two chalices at communing time. To Bishop Seraphim's right, Father Evan Lowig distributes communion.

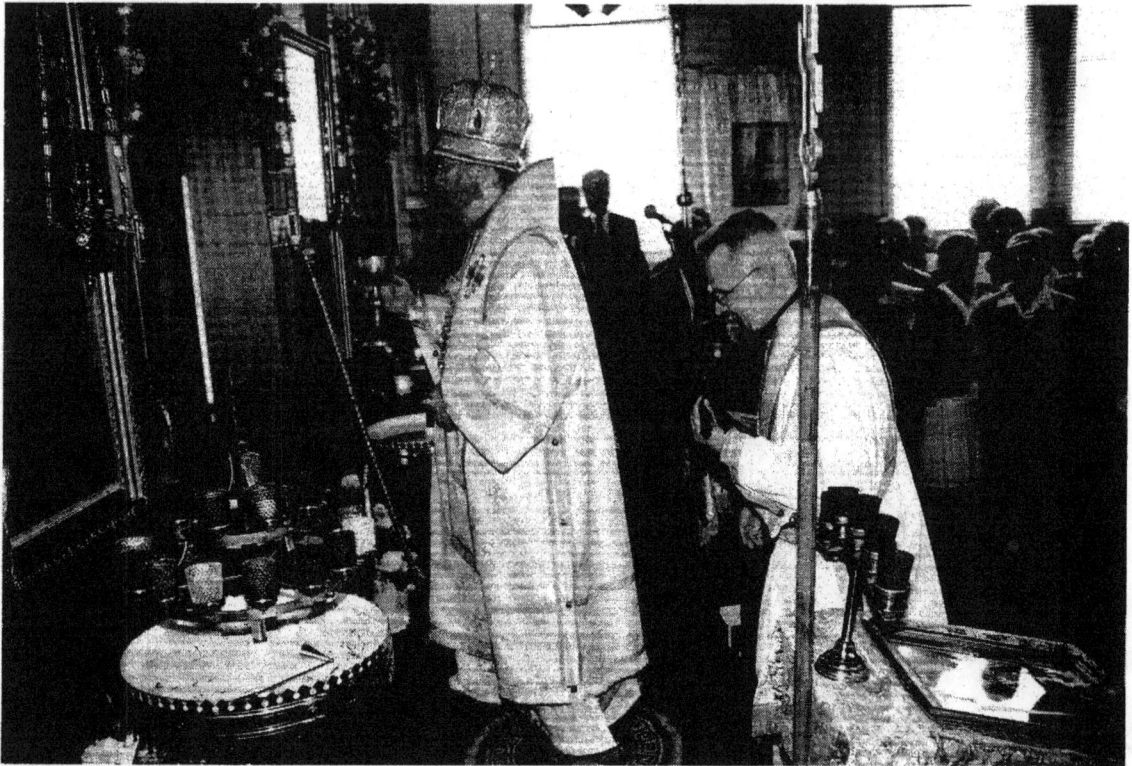

The Communion of the laity finished, Bishop Seraphim and Deacon Andrew Piasta return to the Altar.

Bishop Seraphim about to begin the small blessing of water.

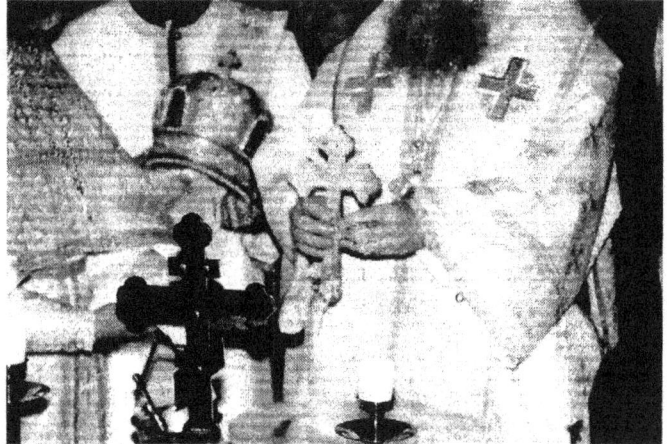

The precious and life-giving Cross of Our Lord Jesus Christ is about to be immersed into the freshly blessed water.

The Bishop now begins the small blessing of water.

Bishop Seraphim takes a sip of Holy Water. The Orthodox Church teaches that this is an important source of sanctification.

The Pontifical Divine Liturgy is about to come to a close.

Bishop Seraphim pronouncing the dismissal.

As part of the dismissal, Bishop Seraphim blesses the congregation
with the Trikiri and Dikiri.

One more invocation of God's blessing upon the gathered flock at
the conclusion of the Divine Liturgy.

Following the Pontifical Divine Liturgy the faithful venerate the
Cross held by Bishop Seraphim and receive the festal anointing
from Fr. Evan Lowig.

The official part of the Divine Liturgy completed as Bishop Seraphim raises the Cross as he gives his final invocation of God's blessing.

The temple being filled to capacity, the faithful slowly make their way outside having venerated the Cross and received the festal anointing

At the conclusion of the Divine Liturgy a procession makes its way to a cairn erected to honor the pioneers of Wostok district during the Centennial of the St. Nicholas Russo-Greek Orthodox Church.

After leaving the church, Bishop Seraphim and concelebrating clergy proceed to the cairn.

The blessing of the cairn is about to take place.

A general view at the site of the cairn while it was being blessed.

Here are members of the processional next to the cairn as they are facing the Bishop and clergy during the special blessing of the cairn.

Here we are in full view of the cairn which is being blessed by Bishop Seraphim. Looking on the large number of congregation and visitors for this celebration.

Bishop Seraphim steps forward to read the prayer for the blessing of a monument.

THE RUSSO GREEK
CATHOLIC ORTHODOX
CONGREGATION OF
ST. NICHOLAS
AT WOSTOK, ALBERTA

Bishop Seraphim blessing the cairn by sprinkling it with Holy Water.

Following the blessing of cairn, the Bishop, clergy and procession move to the cemetery. A memorial service called a, "panachyda" is about to begin. It was served in memorial of all the departed founders and benefactors of the St. Nicholas Church as well as that of Archbishop Sylvester (1914-2000) the ruling Bishop of the Archdiocese of Canada from 1963-1081.) The 3 loaves of bread (Kolachi) are an offering call pomana -- Remembrance.

Bishop Seraphim censing during the panachyda. As we remember the departed our prayer arises as incense and becomes part of the memorial offering.

The parishioners of the St. Nicholas Russo-Greek Orthodox Church of Wostok-Bukowina ---- past and present, living or departed --- stand united in Jesus Christ.

With censer in hand, Bishop Seraphim reads a concluding prayer at the panachyda.

Clergy at the head table for the 100th Anniversary Dinner are:
(L-R) Fr. Vasyl Kolega, Fr. Dennis Pihach, His Grace Bishop
Seraphim, Fr. Evan Lowig, and Deacon Andrew Piasta.

Pictured here is small portion of over 300 guests attending the
festival banquet.

..... more people at the dinner

.... and still more people at the dinner. It was a packed hall and then some!

For the dinner overflow seating was arranged for under a big tent next to the Wostok Hall.

Some of the dedicated women of the parish who prepared the sumptuous meal were: (L-R) Sylvia Halicki, Gladys Gammon, Pearl Shopik, Mary Hunchak, Evangeline Kozakewich and Jackie Hancheruk.

At the gate of St. Nicholas Church you will see this sign post.

A view of the church and cemetery of St. Nicholas Church looking south-west.

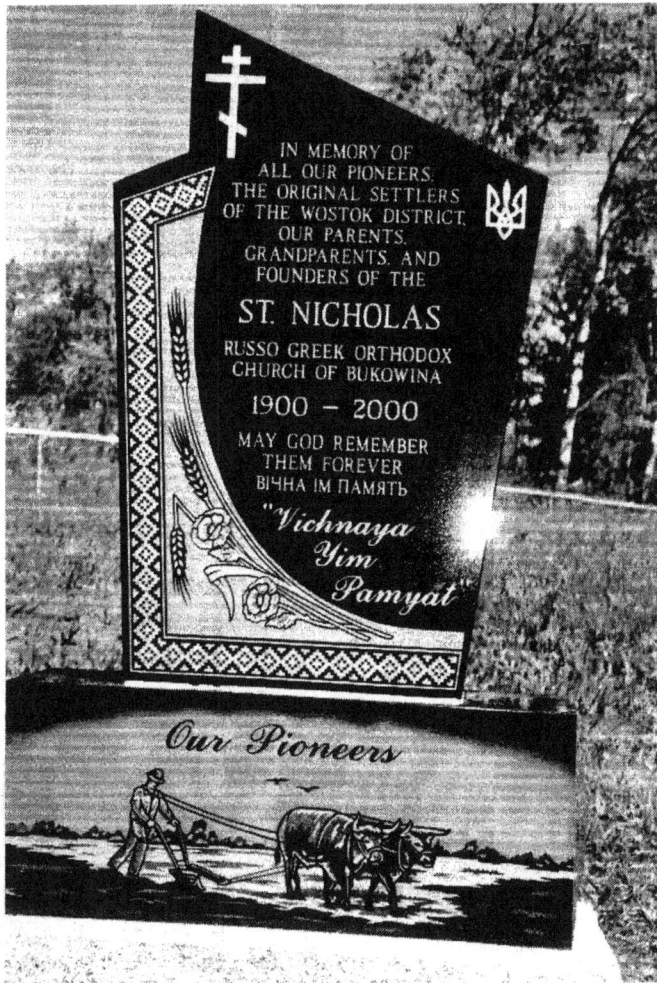

A front view of the commemorative Cairn which identifies and recognizes the founders of St. Nicholas Church.
<<--------

This is the back view of the Cairn.
--------------->>

These are the senior members of St. Nicholas Congregation on June 25, 2000 along with Bishop Seraphim and Fr. Lowig.
Back Row (L-R) : Emma Kubersky, Bishop Seraphim, Rev. Lowig, Mary Olinek, Nancy & Alex Tanasichuk. Front Row (L-R) sitting
are: Cassie Kozakewich, Jennie Wasylynchuk, Katie Wasylynchuk and Florence Kozakewich.

The interior facing the Altar of this beautifully constructed 100-year old church of
St.Nicholas Russo-Greek Orthodox Church of Wostok-Bukowina.

Past priests of St. Nicholas Russo-Greek Orthodox Church of Wostok (Bukowina).

Throughout the years, from 1900 many priests served our church, some served longer, some were supply priests who had but one service. The following is a list of the priests that served us, as can be recalled:

Reverend Alexandr Antoniev
Reverend Gorbachev
Reverend Peter Dowheydo
Reverend Paul Hriczny
Reverend Stefan Verbovy
Reverend Anton Zeminoff
Reverend Nicholas Lewko
Reverend Michael Danilchik
Very Reverend Theodore S. Varchol
Reverend Dmitry Denisiuk
Reverend Chomik
Very Reverend John Kowalchuk
Reverend Wasyl Boyko
Reverend Michael Andruchow
Very Reverend Andrew Kokolsky
Very Reverend Vasily Hochachka
Reverend John Karateew
Reverend Nickolas Germogen
Very Reverend Wasyl Ostashek
Reverend Theodore Gove
Reverend Andrew Morbey
Reverend Larry Reinheimer
Reverend Evan Lowig

Readers Who Served In The St. Nicholas Russo Greek Orthodox Church of Wostok (Bukowina)

George Rechlo
Harry Kudryk
Andrew Emesky
John Yakoweshen
Harry Halkow
Matushka Varchol
Dan Lopushinsky
Myron Cherniak
Wasyl Ostashek
Dmetro Gryskewich
Prokop Tymchyshyn
George Danelesko
Matushka Ostashek
Rose Yakoweshen
John Shandro
Patrick Stewart
Anthony Chilkowich
Deacon Andrew Piasta
Evangeline Kozakewich

www.ingramcontent.com/pod-product-compliance
Lightning Source LLC
Chambersburg PA
CBHW081240090426
42738CB00016B/3361